I ♥ EASTER

Buster Books

Illustrated by Jessie Eckel and Tracy Cottingham

Edited by Helen Brown and Philippa Wingate
Designed by Derrian Bradder

First published in Great Britain in 2018 by Buster Books, an imprint of Michael O'Mara Books Limited, 9 Lion Yard, Tremadoc Road, London SW4 7NQ

The pictures in this book previously appeared in the following books: *The Easter Colouring Book* and *The Easter Sticker and Colouring Book*

With additional material adapted from www.shutterstock.com

[W] www.busterbooks.co.uk   [f] Buster Children's Books   [🐦] @BusterBooks

ISBN: 978-1-78055-577-5

2 4 6 8 10 9 7 5 3 1

This book was printed in February 2018 by Gutenberg Press Ltd, Gudja Road, Tarxien GXQ 2902, Malta.

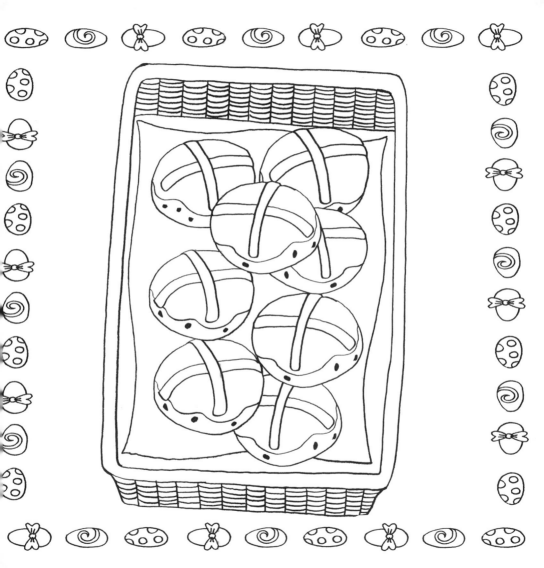

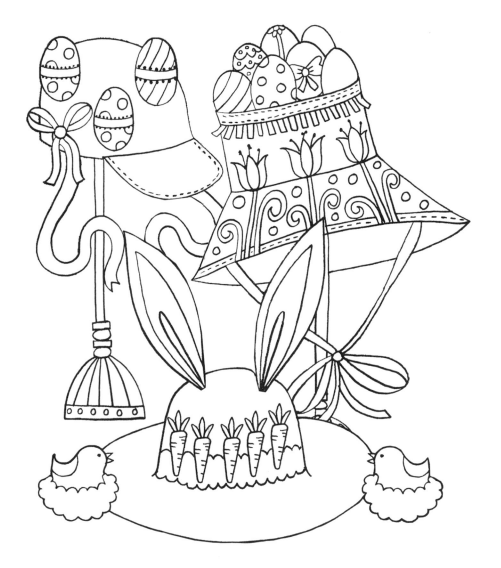

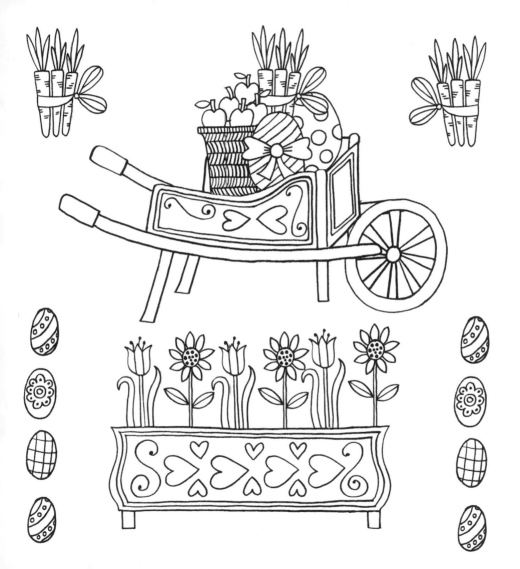

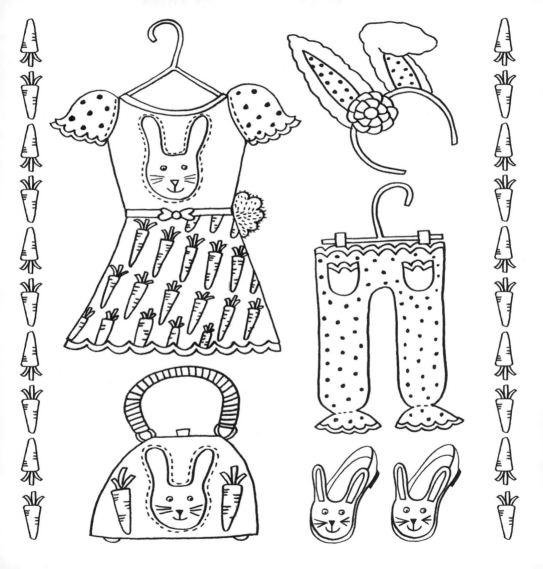

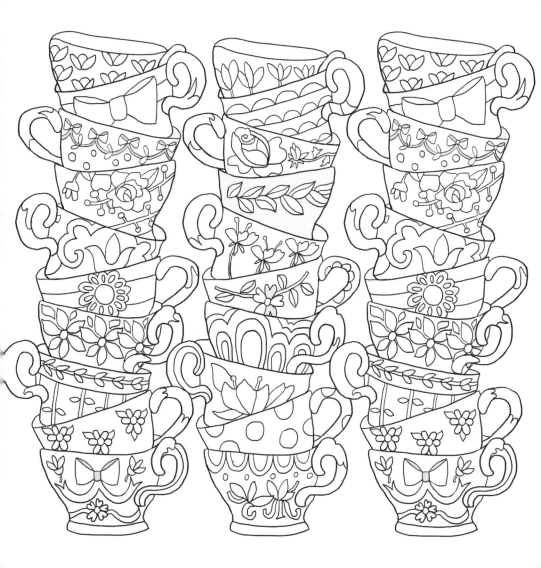